WITHDRAWN

The Place of Understanding

a poem

The Place of Understanding

a poem

by

J. W. Rivers

The PIKESTAFF PRESS

ISBN: 0–936044–06–3

The PIKESTAFF PRESS
P.O. Box 127
Normal, Illinois 61761

Printed in the United States of America

For Mercedes and Francis

Fiammetta and Margarita

also

Elaine and Bill Bruce

Acknowledgments:

Elinor Benedict, David Chorlton, Charlie Farlow, Brian
Meehan, David A. Petreman, Deana Pickard, Francis Rivers,
Norman Rosenfeld, James R. Scrimgeour, Robert D. Sutherland

"In The Woods, The Deer Man Encounters Liza The
Fortuneteller" first appeared as "Hiking With The Old Acorn
Lady" in the July 1988 issue of *Poetry*.

Versions of the following poems from "The Girl Who Dances in
Snow" were featured in the Spring 1993 issue of *The South
Carolina Review*: "1908. Searching for Her Parents, Theresia
Wanders near Heroes' Square"; "Theresia Wants to Leave
Budapest Forever"; "Having Traveled from Budapest to
Eisenstadt, Theresia Meets Herr Schnitzler, the Postmaster,
Whom She Is to Wed by Arrangement"; "Herr Schnitzler Has
Brought Theresia, Five Months Pregnant, to Vienna for a
Fortnight"; "Diary Entry. Late Afternoon Friday following
Corpus Christi Day, 1910"; "Late Spring: Theresia, Eight Months
Pregnant, Stands before Her Husband's Freshly Filled Grave
after the Priest Departs."

The editors acknowledge with thanks the support provided by
the English Department of Illinois State University and by the
Department's Publications Unit in producing this book.

Contents

Part I: The Girl Who Dances in Snow

Part II: The Deer Man

Jewish folklore holds that thirty-six righteous men live in the world at any given time. In this book, Baruch, son of Theresia and grandson of Baruch the Moneylender, is such a *lamed vavnik*. Against the backdrop of the Nazi extermination program, he acts to protect Gypsies as well as his fellow Jews. Mainly, however, he symbolizes the will to resist evil. Historically, the Warsaw Ghetto Uprising of 1943 summoned the attention of a world largely indifferent to the fate of European Jews. On a much more modest level , the words "work slowly and badly" epitomized Jewish opposition to the regimen of forced labor imposed on them by the Nazis. The use of the phrase by Herr Kralik, the SS official, is meant to be satirical. My mockery is directed against Kralik, and I hope that this is clear.

—JWR

Part I

The Girl Who Dances in Snow

❧

...a few untidy Jews, entirely devoted to money-making, and a few Gipsies, who did little honest work, but lived in poverty and squalor....

—Adrian Stokes

Take all the Gipsies that ever came out of the tent, or their descendants...and what are they now? Still Gipsies. They even pass into the other world Gipsies.

—James Simson

Blessed be Jael among women
. . . .
among all women that dwell in tents
may she be blessed.

—The Song of Deborah

Liza the Fortuneteller Warns Magda Grünbaum of the Fate of Her Husband, Baruch the Moneylender, at the Hands of a Mob

(November, 1890
outskirts of Budapest, shortly before a pogrom)

Give me a silver coin, she says, *which you have warmed with your body.*

> *Your husband's breath*
> *Crouches behind mist.*
> *The wind*

> *Snatches it away,*
> *Drags it*
> *Through pistol-whippings and stab wounds.*

> *Beyond limits of smoke and sleep,*
> *Your husband's breath*
> *Rises in the wind,*

> *Seeking the forest of promise,*
> *Soft light in a glade,*
> *Heaven unfurling from its bud—*

> *Finds only*
> *A mapless world*
> *Of claws and fangs.*

> *It seeks a new body—*
> *Fingers to touch a leaf*
> *Or a drop of rain.*

> *Its limbs*
> *Will not learn again*
> *To dress themselves.*

Its eyes are creating
Their own darkness.
Its name does not know itself.

You, Magda, have fattened
Into a housewife,
A cow standing still to be milked.

Packs of wolves
With daggers in their eyes
Are closing in.

Hand me your daughter Theresia.
I will give her
The secret name of Jael;

She will walk the earth
With Gypsies,
Run with yapping dogs and sweating horses.

Her breathing will merge
With the breath of the forest.
She will dance with mice,

Make near the distant birds.
Look: even now
On her forehead

All snow is present in a single flake
As is the coming of Spring
In a bitter green herb.

She spits on the coin and slips it into her sleeve.

Theresia, Who Has Left the Gypsies and Returned to Budapest to find her Parents, Communes with Her Spiritual Mother

circa 1907

Liza, I kiss your hand.

Last week I secured work as a domestic for Frau Heinrich, from Austria. She has given me a pair of ill-fitting boots and a new scrub brush. I am to wash windows and dust the sitting room. But I am not to touch the Virgin Mother. This morning while I was on my knees in the kitchen, her husband smiled, clicked his heels and pulled me to my feet. Looking into my eyes, he gave his sacred word that he would scour synagogues and government offices for traces of my parents, adding that the departed at best have only a small head start. I saw Frau Heinrich come to a stop in the doorway behind him.

Later she sent me to the market for cut flowers. How she must long for the scent and color of once living things. Some well dressed girls, each chaperoned by a governess, came for corsages, giggling about tomorrow's introductions and the wound received last night by so-and-so of the rowing club during a duel in the foyer of the Opera. The funeral is tomorrow, and will be attended by many young men from country estates and university faculties.

When I came back from the market, Frau Heinrich expressed great attachment to me and stated it was her desire that I meet her brother, Herr Schnitzler, a most attractive bachelor who would let me grow lovely flowers in his garden to my heart's content. This is all very unexpected, and I am unsure of such an arrangement....

1908. Searching for Her Parents,
Theresia Wanders near Heroes' Square

She kisses the hand of an old Gypsy
Still playing music from Munkácsy's funeral
Eight years ago.
One thing we know, he says,
Is how to bury the dead.

I want to live in a summer village,
She says, where birds
Play in a garden puddle
And my father's smile brightens the day.

When I was young, he says,
*Artists ground their pigments
And flowers grew in garlands
On Heroes' Square, but November
Came early to bury summer
Beneath a monument, and now they say
That spurts of Jewish blood
Would brighten this small nation.*

I want to run again like a child,
She says, to see how far I can go,
And like a lily be beautiful
Throughout a summer day.

Even in cellars after dark,
He says, *the sun's fading glow
Clung to potted plants, but now
They say that even the Jews
Hate Jews, and Gypsies
Should be driven out.*

I want to go, she says, where the sun
Pulls flowers like tides,
And daylight lasts
Far into the night.

Who would play the music, he asks,
For angels and unicorns
To gambol and chase each other
If the Gypsies were forced back to India?

Down the street, a mob
Is hacking a Jew to pieces.
The Gypsy folds
Theresia into his cloak.

Theresia Wants to Leave Budapest Forever

The moon steals sleep from my eyes
But whispers dreams into my ear
Like my mother's voice
Floating over the river.

Lilies and roses are stuffed
Into flower stalls for the night.
Jews are crammed into Király Street.
Only my thin ceiling holds back
The cold November rain.

In this cramped, airless room
With its dirty straw mattress
I wear a yellow bandage
In which my flesh is ill at ease.

I have eaten my supper of rye bread
With lard and paprika
And cheap yellow wine.
I have no privet hedge for privacy,
No geraniums in a lovely window box,
No father.

Herr Heinrich is now
The city's richest moneylender.
From the other side of my door
Comes a clicking of heels.

It is harder and harder
To live through each day
Than to grow old and mad.
I want to enter another country
And be a doe among wildflowers,
A sunbird tasting nectar.

When all the dogs
And small orchestras are silent,
When taverns and coffeehouses
Have closed their doors,
I will leave the city
Like the Danube slipping away
To set an end to itself.

I will go far from small palaces
And yellow-stuccoed walls,
Where the moon roams through graveyards,
Reading names on stones.

Under a yellow star,
All the names are mine.

Having Traveled from Budapest to Eisenstadt, Theresia Meets Herr Schnitzler, the Postmaster, Whom She Is to Wed by Arrangement

Never speak to foreigners,
He says; *strive to be*
As perfect as the statues.

She talks with ladybugs and crickets.
Do not spread gossip, he says,
About what is not yet known.

Through the window she sees
Autumn colors blanch into winter.

Flowers and leaves
Flare only briefly, he says,
In their fine battle array.
Try to be as beautiful
As the buildings of my city.

She fills a sack with grain.

Do not exhaust your strength
In feeding birds.
You will find them strangely missing
As you chase their tracks through snow,
And you will run
Short of breath on your journey
Back to the door.

She wants to read
Epitaphs in the cemetery.

The language of the stones
Has changed, he says;
In my country, all you need to know
Is what you do,
Weighing in your pitcher
The daily ice of winter
Until your conceits melt away
And your native voice
Shrinks to the size of a hairpin
which bends into your soul.

She sits on the closet floor,
Listening for her breath.

Herr Schnitzler Has Brought Theresia,
Five Months Pregnant, to Vienna for a Fortnight

Inhaling his cigar and fog
As we approach the Café Sperl,
Herr Schnitzler wonders aloud
If the wounds of Christ
Bled as our carriage drove past
The Church of the Nine Choirs of Angels.

As he talks, I dream
Of bathing myself in spring water,
Sleeping with laurel leaves under my head,
Growing as beautiful as my dream come true.

He sees in every park
Snakes that lurk in flowerbeds:
Bearded, dark-skinned men with skull caps
Springing at blond-haired maidens
While streetlamps and stars
Are in hiding behind the fog.

If you are the morning star, Herr Schnitzler,
Keep your light; if you
Are my pulse, be still.
Let me dream
That I wake up in another country
In a gown of butterflies,
In a garden of blossoms and honeybees.

I am the girl who stands in snow
With suet for the birds.
As a child, I dreamed of dancing.
My friends, the Gypsies,
Spoke of men colder than winter,

Which neither could see itself
Nor sweep away the leaves.

Each night I dream, each day
I tremble, waiting for a Gypsy
To warm my feet with his breath
And tell me what
To measure my life against.
I am the girl who stands in snow
With a sack of grain for the birds.

My belly is growing beautiful,
Round with the shape of the world.
I dream of dancing among the trees,
Breathing life into fallen leaves
And naming the world for birds.

Diary Entry
Late afternoon Friday following Corpus Christi Day, 1910

Can I trust my thoughts, ever? They show no clear results.
The taste is never visible of berries on my lips.... Herr
Schnitzler's blue eyes and muttonchops emulate those of the
Emperor. His clothes are cut by English tailors, yet he would
like to leave for work in tunic and feathered hat, flanked by
household guards with panther skins on their shoulders.
Today for breakfast, after another coughing spell, he con-
sumed smoked sausages, Turkish coffee, apricot brandy and
more cigars, looked in spite of weight loss fatter than a
Biedermeier portrait. I feel myself a mere transient in Herr
Schnitzler's house, a night-blooming flower from
Constantinople. With access to his larder, I have no taste for
food. I want to reduce everything to nothing and curl up
inside it. Are sacred names inscribed on new leaves outside?
Does the fish in the water tremble? Is the girl I was still here,
but nowhere to be seen? Will my child be a sacred sheep?
Little that I enter on this page seems down-to-earth, even as
the day, with wings, delivers evening.

Late Spring: Theresia, Eight Months Pregnant, Stands before Her Husband's Freshly Filled Grave after the Priest Departs

Rain is falling like rosary beads.
Alongside his grave, Herr Schnitzler
Argues with the sky.

Standing apart,
I dream myself gaily dressed,
A plump partridge strutting in the sun,
Asking nothing from the earth
But life.

Herr Schnitzler displays on his watch chain
A bullet which flew through his ribs.
Scowling at me across the grave,
He claims that the bullet
Is more constant than the daughters of Abraham,
Who are venomous flies
From a cave in the Carpathians
That poison cattle in Springtime.

> I pulled the dying Herr Schnitzler
> From his featherbed to the floor,
> Rolled him onto my mattress,
> And as I opened the window
> So his soul could escape,
> I felt his coarse hand
> Brushing against my leg.

I want to be nourished by corn
And wine, and ripened in light.
I want to live in the sun,
And rinse my face with dew from the grass.

The bullet, Herr Schnitzler adds,
Clicking his heels,
Is from an accident of the hunt:
Would you like to see
The eyes of a dying deer
Shot full in the throat?

No, I reply,
And I bow my head
To hide my frightened eyes.

I must learn my fate
From a mountain fairy with golden hair
That glitters in moonlight;
Then, like a wild-goose,
Fly with kisses from the Gypsy wind
Floating on my lips.

Wearing a White Babushka, Theresia Makes Ready to Leave Eisenstadt and Go to a Distant Hungarian Forest

A wolf from the desert shall ravage them
—Jeremiah 5:6

THERESIA
(Talking with two angels of God, disguised
as mice, who have befriended her)
If I abide in the house
of the king of wolves
who dresses in claws and fangs,
I must array myself
in flowers and vines,
form a caravan of mice
which travels at night
to a forest garden
and quilt of leaves
under the wings of birds.

MICE
(Jumping over and into each other like
children at play)
Fallow deer and flocks of quail
will join us;
sap will flow in dried-out trees;
fairies in gowns of saffron stigmas
will give us wine
and crush coriander seeds
in tiny mortars for our bread.

THERESIA
(Swaying)
I must lead a march of hopeful mice
beneath the forest vault
where trees and leaves rejoice,

17

and no one dies idly in bed.
     (Pirouetting)
No longer shall we be
as sheep who submit
to the whim of the wolf
or hens who bow down
before the butcher's knife.

    MICE
Are we not all Gypsies
with no country of our own?

    THERESIA
I am the snow-white goose
who will lead you
to the forest of promise.

    MICE
We will breathe the air of dreams
in your hiding-place of the soul.

    THERESIA
Our cries of joy will make a music
of cymbals and tambourines;
we will dance
in the dewy hours of night.

    MICE
Fog can not choke,
hail can not batter,
storm not break
nor fire scorch
the forest of promise.

THERESIA

I shall weave
shawls and sheets and lace
adorned with stars and birds.

MICE

You will make the forest
into a flowery glade
whose creatures will dance
in the sun and falling snow.
Your child's garments
will smell of cinnamon
He will dance
like King David before the Ark
and, like the Gypsy, fall ill
from living in a house.

THERESIA

If the wolf arrives for a bite
I will give him figs
and barley cakes and honey-water.

MICE
(Jumpy)

You must lure the wolf
into a barrel lined with spikes
and roll him down a hill.

THERESIA

I will sit with him among blossoms.
We will sip nectar and sesame wine
and listen to pipes among the flocks.

MICE
You must butcher the wolf,
make sausage of his blood,
headcheese of his paws and heart.

THERESIA
I will embroider pillows
with silken dreams for the wolf,
and bind the windblown sand
with vines and grass.

MICE
Sunflowers will turn
their faces toward you;
at night, old farms
will gleam with fairy-lights.

THERESIA
Rain will sing softly,
water will spring
from the ground into our hands,
flowers will bloom in snow.

MICE
In the center of the holiest place
deep in the forest of promise,
you son will nibble leaves and twigs.

THERESIA
And daily offer up his prayers
to keep in touch with God.

MICE
He will rest with his back to the wind,
sleep in thickets during the day
and roam for food at dusk.

THERESIA
May mountains in his path
dwindle to dust.

MICE
He will don a crown of antlers
to keep the wolf at bay.

THERESIA
His heart will be childlike,
But he will keep an eye
on the ears of the wolf.

As She Trudges Eastward on a Sandy Road, Theresia Envisions Her Mother

Church bells never toll for Jews.

As my mother's head
Lay on the pillow,
Did my father in his shawl
Light a candle?

At her loom she wove
Lilies and saffron
And rose-purple flowers of spikenard
Into cloth.

     Passing through a hollow almond tree
     My mother arrives at the orchard.

     Small animals and trees sing to God.
     Branches and birds hover over her head
     To shade her from the sun.

     My mother gathers honey
     With Ruth and Deborah.

     My mother is the grain
     That sings at harvest.

     She is the perfume
     In God's wine.

In A Gypsy Encampment at the Edge of the Forest

1

Barefoot children are playing
Up to their knees in snow.
Men with violins under their coats
Drink brandy from silver beakers.
From spits and pots, a smell
Of hedgehogs and wild garlic.

Fresh as a stream whose fish
Carry sins to the sea,
The wind arrives
From a country beyond the road,
Turning smoke into open sky.

Bare-legged, Theresia sits
Nursing her baby on a mound of snow.
Between shade and sun lurks the wolf,
She tells the child; its hairy body
Is full of eyes
That grow wide when the moon wanes.

2

Mandori the King of Gypsies appears;
Fairy-lights dance
On the tips of his earrings.

You have come on a sandy road
From the past, he says, *where demons*
Who haunt trees and beds and hurl
Sinners into sizzling pork fat
Pose as obliging members
Of the Burial Society,
As they eye your hair and gold teeth.

But in this place
Small birds and mice
Bring messages from heaven.
Rocks bow down
Before the unseen head of the house.

Long ago, more distant than a lifetime,
The shining face of Moses
Appeared above the clouds
To shepherd deer and mice
Among the innermost rooms of trees,
Far from swirling swords
And gunshots along the roads.

3

To the tuning of the violins
Theresia hums and sways
And dances in slow time.
The air grows sweet with sound,
Which rouses God from sleep:

Tinkers and horse traders sing and play,
He mumbles; *they presume*
To enrich my world through music.

Bearing Tokaj Wine and sparkling water,
Red kerchief around his neck,
God descends with falling snow.

May your horses be long lived,
He greets the Gypsies, *may*
The horizon be always your goal.

4

Men and women and children and God
Promenade on snow;
They sing and play and dance
The night away.

Tomorrow, surrounded
By peacocks and butterflies
The colors of Joseph's coat,
They will drink walnut brandy,
And skip all day
Among flowers and herbs.

God Espies Theresia Nursing Her Baby

In a night
longer than other nights
snow is falling drunkenly.
Gypsy fiddlers sway like angels.

Once, says God, *I walked*
this very place
planting trees,
and now I meet you
in the forest
of my dreams.

Tired of searching
for my father's shawl
and mother's cradlesong,
Theresia says, I come
to kiss the soles
of God's feet
in a world
which I create.

If you do not
dance, he says,
sipping brandy,
you cannot pray.

I am a white dove
before a temple of snow.
I have seen that clouds,
water-ripples,
birds and men
vanish while God
goes dumbly about
kindling festival lights.

God comes here,
he says, *to draw*
strength from flowers,
from vines that rise up
in prayer higher than himself
and trees whose language
is in words they never utter.

    In the moment that I have
    I want to see
    white squirrels,
    deer grazing
    in white pastures,
    mice raising their heads
    in sun and snow.

And I who have walked
among figures of stone
and salt and cities
blasted by the ram's horn
seek a point in time
where I may purchase quiet.

    Only the Gypsies,
    scattered like Jews,
    whose maps
    are wagon ruts,
    have kept at their table
    an extra cup for me.

To look for light
in darkness and listen
for rumors of angels
spreading among trees
in a silence
as sure as night

is to make my spirit
dance when I cannot see
the path beyond my feet.

I do not know
the inner life of God,
but when the moon
emerges from his hand
to light up eternity,
I want to speak to him
by dancing.

The Gypsies have fallen asleep,
Their dreams before them
In sunny Spain and Italy.

The music of far-off birds
And the smell of tomorrow's flowers
Fill Theresia's mind.

At the tabernacle
God cuddles the baby.
Theresia dances in snow
In the forest of endless dreaming.

Carrying Her Infant Son Baruch, Theresia Wanders through the Forest and Stops to Kneel at a Frozen Pond

Squirrels are examining
Hidden glyphs on bark
And giving voice to ancient tongues.

Theresia kneels on a flat stone.
The sun
Halts in the sky as she sings to Baruch

> Behold smiling grapes
> and temples
> of muskrats and beaver.

> Trickles of water
> bring mountains to their knees,
> but wooden temples and Gypsy tents

> stand up to the wind.
> Gypsy souls
> pierce the sky like birds

> chasing the horizon
> above roads that by day
> lie still

> and go their way at night.
> When ice in the streambed melts
> and Gypsies pour onto the road,

> you and I will build
> a hermitage of toadstool huts
> with tapestries of grass and vines . . .

The sound
Of clicking heels in the distance
Cuts short her singing.

Leaving Baruch with a herd of deer,
She drifts
Like a dream through the forest.

At the silent camp,
Scattered around
Pig iron potbelly stoves,

Men and women and children
With red bubbles at their throats
Stare at the sun.

> *I have scoured synagogues*
> *and Gypsy campsites,*
> Herr Heinrich says,

> *looking constantly for you*
> *so that we may arouse*
> *tomorrow's dreams today.*

Smiling,
He clicks his heels
And steps toward her.

She rams
A tent-peg
Through his neck.

Theresia Mourns the Loss of Her Friends

Her milk has stopped.

Buckets, blankets and wagons
Are dissolving into ashes.
Worms eat rugs and armchairs.

Shadows without heads
Lie in wait for Theresia.
She sees the wolf, who tears
The fetus from a living doe.

On a white branch
An angel appears as a dove:

You have tasted
the dew of life,
my daughter,
and danced the dance
of human hope.

I reach like willow roots
for the damp soil
of the grave, she says;
would reach out
my neck to the knife
to join the Gypsies
in their cold exile with God.

Already your son's soul
is expanding
to wrap its arms
around the forest.
Like King Solomon,

he is learning
the language of birds
and he coaxes
rain from the sky.

A doe steps forth
To suckle Baruch.
Fawns lick his flesh.

An unseen road
Becomes visible in Theresia's mind.
At the far end,
Dressed as night-club musicians,
God and the Gypsies are playing
Violins in the snow.

Theresia dances toward them,
Taking the road with her.

Part II
The Deer Man

ॡ

In the far forest the lad heard,
at once he jerked up his head,
with his wide nostrils testing
the air...

—Ferenc Juhász

Every man affects the fate of the world through his whole
being and all his acts, to a degree unknown both to him
and to others.

—Martin Buber

Just wait, you matzoh-eating people,
The night of the long knives is coming.

—Horst Wessel Lied

We are still searching for our fathers, in whose presence
we were always children, and for our mothers . . .

—Sándor Scheiber

Psychoanalyst's Clinical Chart Entry Regarding the Deer Man, Detained by Worshippers in the Seitenstettengasse Synagogue

Vienna
August 17, 1937

Barefoot and clad in a cloak of his own hair, he was dancing on the central desk, sprinkling ashes of small animals, his lips moving but making no sound. Rabbi Feldschreiber had him removed to my consulting room, where on the couch he now dreams that his wetnurse was a doe whose flesh was torn by the wolf, that with the aid of Heaven he slew a dozen soldiers in a smoldering forest. From far off, birds brought him seeds and berries; mice, small crumbs of bread. He dreamed a sandy road on which he fled to Vienna, where he has transferred to me a pouch containing a dozen foreskins. I have placed them in formaldehyde.

August 18. In Psychoanalysis, the Deer Man Remembers Footprints that Kill

Followed by rumors
Of wailing women,
Leather boots are trampling
Flowers along the road.

> *Who lives here?*
> the captain demands.
> I do, I tell him;
> my home
> is this very soil
> beneath my feet.

The captain smiles,
And shells ignite the forest;
The wooden temple
Fills with a great light.

Deer run in circles.
Squirrels scamper up
Trees as old as God.
Roots crouch in their cellars.

Earth recoils
From the weight of guns
As soil shrinks back
From the harrow's teeth.

> *Only men feel pain,*
> the captain asserts.
> *Dirt is only dirt,*
> *trees are merely trees.*

The clarity of fire
Lends him the form of the wolf.
Henbane sprouts up
In his footprints.

My life is silent.
I feel weighted down
By nothing.

Clinical Chart Entry, August 19

He sees the pebbles of my aquarium as living things. The fish
allow him to stroke them. At the window he finds a wasp,
takes it in hand, forces the screen and returns the wasp to
the open air. He looks at my daughter Anna as if through a
mist made up of dewdrops; she hears in the mist a music of
cornets and timbrels. I sense that I must help him divide up
ashes in a sacred place, restore the walls of a forest. He has
confronted the wolf. It is our turn soon.

Anna Tells Her Father of a Picnic with the Deer
Man in the Vienna Woods Earlier in the Day

He sniffed wild cyclamen, pulled fluffy dumplings from the basket, gulped down the raspberry soup, spilling drops on his shirt.

A formation of brown uniforms marched by—average men who, like locusts, want to lay waste to the world and thus forget themselves. They stared at my companion's sturdy shoulders and russet hair. The hiking clothes you lent him gave him the look of a Swiss Alpinist.

Why not come and drill with us? the leader asked him. The others leered at me and sang, *Just wait, you hook-nosed people, the night of the wolf is coming.*

In the forest, the Deer Man replied, *each form of life finds its own place. At this time of year, reptiles slither forth only in rain, or after sundown.*

November, 1938. A Coachman Flogs His Rearing Horse

"It isn't the way it used to be," said one leaf to
the other.

"No," the other leaf answered. "So many of us
have fallen off to-night we're almost the only ones
left on our branch."

"You never know who's going to go next," said
the first leaf.

—Felix Salten

The Deer Man springs forward,
Seizes the whip,
Whispers into the horse's ear,

Then rebukes the coachman:
Horses are gifts from God.

Only a Gypsy would say that,
Monsignor Karpfen snorts,
Stepping from the coach.

His name is Mischa,
The Deer Man says;
Once he was a Gypsy
Who did not love music.
He is paying for his sin.

Gypsies are as shifty
As the Jews who murdered God,
The monsignor sneers;
This animal should be
Rendered into dog food.

The Deer Man lashes the priest
Across the cheek:
The scar will be
Your mark of grandeur.
Tell your bishop you acquired it
In a fight to the death
With Hungarian Jewish mercenaries.

Leaves hang in the air
By fragile veins.

From around the corner,
Breaking glass
And the crackle of fire.

Spring, 1939. In the Woods, the Deer Man Encounters Liza the Fortuneteller

She sees rocks release
Ancient reserves of moonlight
And bathes herself in the glow,
Hears frogs pray for rain,
Sees corn and beans in bloom
Where I see only straw.
A smell of mushrooms
Is in her clothes.
She hears a beating of wings,
Voices from water and peonies.

Put all that you are, she says,
Into the least thing you do.
All that has been
And all that has been said
Still reaches us
If we watch the road
And listen to the trees.
Squirrels chatter
In ancient languages,
A moon can rise
From behind a flower.
You will capture
The wind with your hair,
The sun with your eyes,
And balance your burden
So it is light.

I hear leaves around us
Reciting prayers
As her breath grows cold
And shrinks
To the length of her thumb.

Gypsies come out of shadows
To seal her eyes with cobwebs,
Sprinkle her lips with pollen.
Soon she will arise,
Bringing her whole life with her.

How Sara Met God, Who Foretold
the Coming of Baruch, a Righteous Man

I said nothing,
only sat and looked at him
And let him look at me.

Then: Would you like
To sit by the fire?
I have some bread and wine.

He settled himself on the ground
And said to me:
Granddaughter of Liza the Fortuneteller

Who gathers grapes and honey
In the sun
And visions

In the dark,
Be your peace always great
Among passing shadows of friends.

I spat three times
Into the stream,
Then gave him bread and wine

From the wagon, saying
The Lord's name be praised
In the twelve hours of light,

Be it also praised
During the twelve hours
Of night—may the Lord

Live a thousand years.
With his sleeve be wiped
Crumbs from his beard, then spoke:

I met once a woman
From whom mice did not run
But nestled in her lap;

Birds with bells in their throats
Sought her shoulder.
As dew is the promise

Of life for the grass,
Her son comes now
In the prenatal light of early dawn,

Moving easily across borders
From a distant forest
Where birds made of mud

Sleep in dead trees.
He comes to fast all day
And pray at night,

To plant trees
In order to climb them
And invoke voices from the leaves.

Getting up, he placed
His hands on my head:
You must pare your nails

And shave yourself.
I grant you the consent
Of one hundred rabbis.

Some mice scurried into his robe.
As he walked, he left
Footprints on rocks.

Sara Waits for Baruch

She sits on a campstool.

The Deer Man follows
A faint harmony
Of psalteries and flutes
Until the tent appears.

The music you hear,
She says, is in your head.

*With a sip of water
And a Gypsy tune,* he replies,
I can soon be drunk.
He kisses her hand.

You inhabit a forest
Of music in your brain,
She says, like a man who lives
On a mountain with birds.

He gazes at the sky.
*My thoughts are bound in moonlight;
I dream of a woman
Who dispels gloom through song.*

Yahweh's spirit is upon you,
She says, but
Is a man without a beard
Not a eunuch?

*I seek a road I once walked;
I wish now,* he says, *to see it again
For the first time.*

She pours water into a silver goblet:
Such a road opens, she says,
In the moonlight of the mind,
Where Gypsies
Cure the sick through music.

He follows the road
Into her tent.

Baruch and Sara Have Just Finished Snacking
on Cheese and Radishes

> ...for we were men who could defend the State in
> time of war and must have been a highly gifted
> people to have been thus slain during twenty centu-
> ries and yet to be alive.
>
> —Theodor Herzl

1

Dried by the sun,
Garlands of mushrooms
Hang from branches.
Garlic is strung to a tent pole.

Using an oak stump for a breadboard,
Sara rolls strudel dough
As thin as a veil.
In a glazed pot
Baruch stores dark-red strawberries.

Notes from their singing
Linger among birds in the air:
When wolves are as grazing sheep
And Gypsies have spread their tents
Like snow over the world,
We will know our children
And give comfort to our parents....

2

Snow absorbs the tent
And the backs of the horses.

A bearded man in faded gaberdine
And round, black hat appears:

I have been walking
In a waking dream
Where fevers pollute the air,
Demons cast unwary travelers
Into vats of boiling semen
And wolves rampage through streets.
Is this the forest of promise
I have been looking for?

Sara points to the wagon:
Come and rest, old man;
There is room for every stranger.
Hear music
To relieve your pain.

Baruch takes him by the arm:
Travelers in this place
Are shielded by God.
Come, I will bathe your feet.

Echoes reach them
Of pistol-whippings
And groans from stabbings.
The birds freeze in their flight.

Sipping Demitasse and Cognac, Monsignor Karpfen Acquaints the Nuncio with Events in the Vienna Woods

Lieutenant Lange was a countertenor.
I baptized him myself.
He always said that singing
Was better than talking, and claimed
That generals meet the enemy
Only on maps.
Last week his body was found,
Throat adorned
With a thin red necklace.

How offensive to good taste,
The nuncio remarks,
Eating plum tart.
Purple jam
Oozes down his chin.

Major Menger danced smartly
With his bride at their wedding.
The children are growing
Blue-eyed, tall, and blond.
Yesterday his foreskin,
Strung from a branch above his body,
Dangled in the breeze,
And his hands
Had been lopped off.

The Führer contends that war is life,
War is the origin of all things,
The nuncio declares
From behind a custard cream puff.

The monsignor goes on:
Only one man
Knows the woods like a deer.
He lives in a thicket with a she-goat,
Nibbles leaves and twigs
And rests with his back to the wind.
Bats are snarled in his hair.
He talks to horses and rats,
Eats hearts and brains of children
Whose blood glows in his cheeks.

The nuncio reaches for more pastry.
A hand flies through
The open window
And lands on the tray.

In a Coffeehouse Opposite Hofburg Palace

> (Echoes of waltzes hover in the air. Mahogany mirrors give onto ornate platters and tiered cookie trays, multiplying and transforming pastries into chiaroscuro zones of petits fours, tortes and coffee cakes. Prim waitresses stand ready to serve. Two men, one with a monocle, speak in low tones.)

BARUCH
(Disguised in a stolen black uniform with death's-head insignia.)
So Himmler himself has sent you?

KRALIK
To find a solution to the Gypsy Question. Would you recommend the marzipan dates?

BARUCH
I recommend the poppy seed strudel.

KRALIK
(Selecting sourcream cake.)
Who is this so-called wild man of the woods who wants to keep alive the will to resist?

BARUCH
A monster of alien blood who commits atrocities.

KRALIK
You have seen him?

BARUCH
He holes up among evil spirits, gravediggers, Jews and witches.

KRALIK

Why has he not been disposed of?

BARUCH

Made visible by dance, his steps and gestures are as various as
lights in a forest.

KRALIK
   (In a burst of fury, he flails with his swagger
   stick at an apricot glaze cheesecake.)
But we are in a city ruled by reality and truth, not mere
music!

BARUCH

He prowls barefoot at night, disappears through small doors
in trees.

KRALIK

Naturally.

BARUCH

He is a shadow in a wine cellar. . . .

KRALIK

Of course.

BARUCH

A flitting phantom on the Ringstrasse, dancing with fairies in
moonlight.

KRALIK

Without doubt.

BARUCH

How will you deal with such a monster?

KRALIK

He is nothing but a Jew with the heart of a grasshopper. His mother took up with Gypsies and lived unrestrained in a forest. When I tell him who and what he is, he will come apart.

BARUCH

He will tremble, of course, and grow deadly faint.

KRALIK

The hawk will dive upon the rabbit.

BARUCH

He will scream and pull out his hair.

KRALIK

I will let him run upon his own bayonet.

BARUCH

What? Not give him a sporting chance?

KRALIK
(Licking his swagger stick.)
Of course. I will order pistols for two and coffee for one.

BARUCH

Herr Kralik, before you confront such a creature, fill your pockets with salt, walk backward to a crossroads and pray to God before the garlic on your breath turns black.
(He rams his fist through Kralik's monocle.)

The Temptation of Monsignor Karpfen

The smell of roasting lamb enters a chamber. The monsignor, weak from fasting since midafternoon, meditates with his head between his knees, contemplates a cross, chants hymns. Outside the monastery, bells summon the wind.

In the dining hall, lamb is being sliced, wine is being poured. The monsignor sees himself leading a Crusade through Palestine, putting infidels to the sword, catapulting into besieged cities heads of prisoners and rotting carcasses of horses, wading through massacres and singing Te Deums with tears of ravishment, distributing to his Crusaders the body of Christ in stale crumbs.

Clergy are stuffing themselves with lamb and quaffing wine. In faroff Palestine, the monsignor takes a mouthful of wine from an antique grail. As he rolls it around in his mouth, he hears birds singing songs of praise, sees someone in a babushka and white linen robe leading a procession of doves and mice through a snowy forest.

In a Gutted Synagogue in Leopoldstadt

Rabbi Shlomo Feldschreiber
Takes shape.

To not offend the ears
Of passers-by outside,
He chants
Softly in the dark.

Still searching for our fathers
to be with them
at the time of their death,
we are here for barely a day
to study, offer prayers and die.

Baruch appears before him:
I come to the mohel
On the eighth day
Of my eighth month in Vienna
To become truly attached to God.

Over fragments of decanters
The rabbi intones a blessing
And lights a twisted candle stub.

Moses my teacher
who brought down on Egypt
vermin the size of eggs
bids me advise you, my son,
that God meets his people
in the forest.

Doves descend from a rafter
And coo into their ears.

Scanning faces in the past,
Their eyes smile through
The starlight of a shared dream.

Beholding Abraham
Radiant in the sky,
The rabbi fades from view.

Alone, by candlelight,
Swaying before tambourines and flutes,
Baruch circumcises himself
With a fragment of glass.

At SS Headquarters

Wearing gloves,
Herr Kralik dangles
Mandori's head by its hair.

In the camps this King of Gypsies
Worked slowly and badly,
Emulating a Jew, but now
His debt is paid and justice done.

Baruch and Sara slip in through a window.
With daggers they descend on Kralik.

From the hall
Shouts invade the room.
Seizing Mandori's head, Sara
Bounds through the window
Followed by Baruch.

On wings of smoke
Guards with guns
Pursue them down the streets.

In Schönbrunn Park the soldiers
Come upon a dove
and two terra cotta deer
Glistening from a forest downpour.

Epilogue: The River of Light

God dwells in his tent
In the center of the forest,
Resting his feet on an ark.

Holding hands,
Jewish and Gypsy children
Follow a cloud shaped like a pillar.

How can we find our fathers?
A little boy asks
In the language of deer.

Even shadows search for each other,
another boy replies.

We must bathe
In the rainbow,
A little girl says,
To behold faces in the past.

Birds with bells in their throats
Are talking to the living
About the dead.

Wearing a skull cap,
God mixes sunlight with mist
To cleanse the children from sin.

A river flows from the tent,
Bathing the children to their bones.

God rests his feet
In the tent
On the far side
Of light.

A Brief Glossary

Jael

> A woman of the Kenites, a desert clan in the kingdom of Israel around the 12th century BC. She killed Sisera, a Canaanite general, by driving a tent peg through his temple as he lay asleep in her tent.

Juhász, Ferenc

> The epigraph in Part II of this book is from his "The Boy Changed into a Stag Cries Out at the Gate of Secrets." See *Modern Hungarian Poetry*, edited by Miklós Vajda, Columbia University Press, New York, 1977. English translation by Kenneth McRobbie.

mohel

> 'Circumciser' in Hebrew. Procedure takes place usually on 8th day following birth; in adult males, it is done prior to any formal conversion to Judaism.

Salten, Felix

> A Viennese Jew from whose book *Bambi* the leaf epigraph in Part II of this book is taken.